Rumors of
Beauty
and
New Beginnings

Wayne William Snellgrove
Fishing Lake First Nation

BLUE FORTUNE ENTERPRISES LLC

RUMORS OF BEAUTY AND NEW BEGINNINGS

For information contact:

Blue Fortune Enterprises, LLC
Aster Press
P.O. Box 554
Yorktown, VA 23690
http://blue-fortune.com

Cover Photography by Tony Montagano

Cover design by Blue Fortune Enterprises, LLC

ISBN: 978-1-961548-29-9

First Edition: July 2025

This book is dedicated to all Sixties Scoop survivors —
especially to those who never found their way
back to the Red Road.
You are not forgotten.

1.

In the realm of the Spirit,
Life begins when courage takes hold.

2.

Looking internally with a connection to the medicine
creates a new, healthy perspective.

3.

It's a beautiful consciousness that connects us all,
love. In my experience, most do not take the time to
understand their connection to those things that bring
us life. That is the beginning of love. Until they do, there
is only misunderstanding.

4.

We suffer from the hate that we offer as much as the
love that we withhold.

5.

The healer understands the healing process
is never complete.

6.

The journey of abundance:
understanding abundance is the ability and capacity to
turn knowledge into wisdom.

7.

Finding, hearing, feeling, and seeing the heart of all things begins with our relationship with Mother Earth.

8.

Medicine Wheel teaching:

The land teaches us consistently
how to conduct ourselves.

9.

Worrying about other people's perception of
who you are is a waste of time.

10.

Medicine Wheel Teaching:
Being a water protector begins within,
healing our own unresolved trauma.

11.

Life. Life is most important.
Awareness of life.
Connection to Earth.
Conscious of frequency.
Sensitive to vibration.
This means we can live a single lifetime
in every moment.
A single breath. Every heartbeat.

12.

Two-fold offering:

One: Our life is a gift from the Creator.
An offering of life to us.
Two: We must use this offering for the
next seven generations.

13.

Life. Let us be grateful for today's offering.
We are supposed to share this life offering with others:
love and light.

14.

The energies of Earth mirror our internal bodies. When we connect with those medicines, plants, fire, and water stones, we align with our physical and spiritual health.

15.

Every day, life gives us four things: lessons, happiness,
experience, or memories.
It is our choice to decide which.

16.

One must always be ready.
Not be tense but to show and be compassion.
Day or night. Any season.

17.

There is no other—only us.
We are everything and everything is us.
The only time we have is now.
There is no death, only life and existence.

18.

Consciousness is a living, breathing entity. It has a
memory. A vibration. A sound. A frequency. A history.
It runs through all natural things.
It knows no time or space.
It only knows now.

19.

If you are the wind,
why are you worried about the breeze?
If you are ocean,
why are you worried about the puddle?
If you are the mountain,
why are you worried about the hill?
If you are the universe,
why are you worried about anything?

20.

To understand love is to know that we can remain calm, peaceful, and compassionate in the storm.

21.

Investing in Love begins with peace, love and gratitude.

22.

Love is understanding that there are no others.

23.

Our trauma in relationship to our healing dictates that
to be alone is okay. But we must learn to be okay with
being alone without being lonely.

24.

Our relationship to the Spirit and Spiritual matters like love, anger, fear, compassion, resentment, and greed will dictate the house we live in, the thoughts we think, how we live, and the conduct of our relationships.

25.

Only after being alone with time and truth
can wounds turn into wisdom.

26.

The universe needs one thing from you:
the daily transition from the old you to the new you.

27.

Medicine Wheel teaching:
We only learned from yesterday.
Don't compare to yesterday, last week,
last month or late year.

28.

Our choices:
Our healthy or unhealthy attachments are our offerings
to the following generations.

29.

Every cell in our body is the universe.
The universe is listening and responding to
every word and thought we say.

30.

There are no tests in life, only choices.
These choices lead to lessons.
If learned, these lessons lead to new beginnings.
We all have an opportunity for a new beginning.

31.

Earth is a living being.
We are living beings.
When we heal, the Earth is healing.
When we forgive, the Earth heals.

32.

Our prayer is not here to change the world but to create
a new relationship with ourselves.

33.

Our ancestors haven't gone anywhere;
we welcome them, honor them, and love them
through the words, prayers, and love we carry.
If we don't feel close to them, it is not them who left;
it's us.

34.

Our frequency is already within us. Our prayers and our words are our connection to them.
Our organs = frequency.

35.

Emotional = vibrations
Mental = frequency

36.

The elements are there to help open our consciousness.
Not raise our frequency but to connect to them.

37.

That place between the prayers and the fear, the silence and the words, decides our future and our offering to the next seven generations.

38.

Mother Nature is always available to take away the noise the rest of the world offers and reduce it to silence.

39.

Mother Earth, the Stars, the Ancestors, and all other life offer beautiful opportunities to grow and learn. Imagine if you could, you started today to take these opportunities up. What would your life look like tomorrow, next week? Next month. Next year?

40.

We can quickly gauge what's happening within us by
the company we allow around us,
people, places, and things.

41.

Awareness. Please do not focus on what is happening around you first, but on what's happening within... What we allow within us is represented by what we allow around us.

42.

When we forgive any person, place or thing,
Mother Earth feels it. And she heals.

43.

Our ancient ancestors did not have therapy other than the seasons, trees, rivers, oceans, fire, moonlight, sun, mountains, rain forest and deserts.

44.

Life:
There are no lessons. Only choices. We are searching for our memories of how to live a good life.

45.

Let gentleness be our default mode.
Let forgiveness be our default mode.
Let standing up again be our default mode.
Let helping others be our default mode.
After, we will begin to understand what love is.

46.

If we cannot self-examine, we cannot understand love.

47.

If I cannot grow, it isn't love

48.

The real power is understanding our experience.

49.

Our helpers aren't separated from us and never were.
They are sitting with us right now. We only need to be
grateful to begin this beautiful relationship.

50.

We have to check in frequently,
or we automatically check out.

51.

Understanding a prayer:
Prayer is repetition. Prayer is preparation.

52.

Peace is found at the center of all things.

53.

The irony of fate is we always end up
where we need to go.

54.

The simple recognition and honoring the first of every
day is essential.
Gratitude for our first breath.
Gratitude for our life.
Our first words.
Our first prayers.
Our first sip of water.
Our first time welcoming the sun.
We are welcoming the return of our ancestors.

55.

The Magic of living a healed life is found in those things you're avoiding.

56.

Those Nations who do not speak still have a beautiful language. Humanity must learn to connect to the unspoken languages.

57.

We have come to a place of healing when we treat ourselves like the next seven generations.

58.

Every single lie, no matter how small, affects our spiritual awareness, what and how we see.

59.

This way, courage and stupidity are somewhat similar,
and both will hurt.
But the difference is that courage is learning the lesson.

60.

People get into relationships by understanding their truth. If they can't listen or understand the truth of their reality, how can they possibly appreciate yours?

61.

I = We
We = Consciousness
Consciousness = I

62.

Destiny finds us when we charge into our greatest fears.

63.

States of consciousness lie mainly in our connection to
the Medicines of Mother Earth.

64.

Medicine Wheel teaching:
Sacred center is connection.
Connection = consciousness.
Consciousness is life.
Life is connection.

65.

How we love ourselves is
how we show others to love us.

66.

There is no strength without courage.
There is no courage with vulnerability.

67.

How you fall in love with the healing process is by
showing others to love themselves.

68.

We are the prayers we walk with.

69.

The animals tell the health of the Earth.

70.

Love is an emotion that has to be expressed
spiritually, emotionally, and physically.

71.

Alone isn't the feeling that you don't have anybody.
It's that sinking feeling that no one has you.

72.

Holy land is everywhere, from the center of the universe to the center of Mother Earth.

73.

Often, we have to cry to learn to breathe.
Crying is a part of learning how to balance and cleanse
with breath and water.

74.

Without Imagination, knowledge is nearly useless.
Knowledge with Imagination is
the creativity that transforms.
And it can transform perspective into reality.

75.

Truth:
Turtle Medicine teaches only true wealth and abundance create a better world for the next seven generations.

76.

The greatest gift and healing we can offer the next seven generations is to find a way to love ourselves.

77.

The highest form of prayer is walking, living, and
sharing the ways of Mother Earth.

78.

Cultural and racial harmony begin with our
relationship with Mother Earth.

79.

Prayer is that spiritual and physical place of
how we walk after we pray.

80.

Who we are as a culture and as individuals is
a clear history of our prayers.

81.

We are from the Stars but so are all plants and animals,
and we are seeded here on Earth to become
beautiful and better people.

82.

Intention is your choice.
Prayers are intentions.
Intention is our choice.
Choice dictates the way we walk, understand,
and look at the world.

83.

Greed is a commitment to poverty, and it relates a commitment to a spiritual agreement to poverty.

84.

How can one understand the world
they fail to listen to?

85.

Shamanism is only a word. But a prayer isn't something we do or a place we go — it's who we are. And the way we walk to our future ancestors.

86.

We must learn to listen to those things that bring and connect us to life. Air, water, fire, and Earth.

87.

Indigenous success is walking with the ways of Earth.

88.

Love so deeply you don't have to forgive.
Only respect the journey.

89.

Just as the Earth is lent to us by our children,
our life is lent to us by the future seven generations.

90.

The highest form of offering prayers is singing.
The highest form of receiving a prayer is listening.

91.

Humility and truth are the great purifiers.

92.

The closer we get to the sickness,
the more labels we use.
The further away from the sickness,
the closer to humanity we are.

93.

The Buffalo understands respect so deeply it gives all.

94.

The highest form of prayer and love is listening
to those who have come before you.

95.

Medicine Wheel teaching:
When we offer and pray to the Bear Spirit, we are not
only communicating with the one but to the collective.
We are heard by millions, every Bear that has ever been.

96.

The old saying, "The only thing that changes is everything," is true. Mother Earth is rotating. Moon phases, tide in and out, seasons, everything. Deeper understanding comes when we step into physical changes and spiritual motions that flow around us; without these, we will remain static.

97.

If we forget, we are in a ceremony,
we will forget we are sacred.
If we forget we are sacred,
we will forget Mother Earth is sacred.
If we forget Mother Earth is sacred,
we will fail to treat each other as sacred.

98.

Consciousness begins with conscious awareness.

99.

Grandmother Moon and Father Sun have
known all our ancestors.

100.

It's not a power we are looking for. It's a connection.

101.

Those lessons we take and carry with us
are the ones that matter most.

102.

It is what we learn and walk with by sacred law
that resonates with future generations.

103.

Confidence isn't if they like me.
It's what I think of myself when they don't.

104.

Confidence is built not on people's judgements or opinions but on the prayers of natural law we hold.

105.

Mother Earth is teaching us how to
live with and in the Universe.

106.

Life:
Everything is about love and our relationship with it.

107.

There is no such thing as religion,
only alignment with Natural Law.

108.

The one who looks for and finds faults in others is the one who hasn't examined their faults yet.

109.

The people are becoming sick because
they don't use words in a sacred way.
When people don't use words in a sacred way,
they will forget these words.
When they forget these words,
they will fail to treat each other in a sacred way.
If they forget to treat each other in a sacred way,
they will fail to treat Mother Earth in a holy way.

110.

Like healing and connection,
understanding the truth is a process.

111.

We may not remember the love the ancestors had
for us, but they still remember.

112.

The truth isn't about reminding someone of theirs
but reminding you of yours.

113.

Lack of confidence in one's self deletes the one person who can genuinely help you: yourself.

114.

The seven laws are connected to our relationship with Mother Earth. Our confidence relationship is also directly related to the seven laws and Mother Earth.

115.

Healed people hear and see things differently.

116.

"We love you" means that we know that you are sacred.

117.

I meet the Creator when I sit with humility, truth, love, honesty, wisdom, respect, and courage.

118.

The love we offer is the absolute connection
we have with Mother EARTH.

119.

Our love is strengthened by our deepened relationship
with those things that offer us life—the elements,
Earth and Stars, straight to the center of
the Mother and universe.

120.

Greed is a foolish man's glory.

121.

Creator and Mother Earth saved me from their god,
religion, and especially the Bible.

122.

The ceremony is about finding our way home.

123.

Medicine Wheel Teaching:
We are all healers.

124.

Hate and anger never sleep.
Gentleness and compassion make the best pillows.

125.

Living the way of sacred natural law connects us to all directions: the ancestors and the future.

126.

Seven Grandfather Teachings:
Our safe place, sacred place, and protection
are these sacred laws.

127.

Often it is only the silence that separates us.

128.

Without Natural Law or our connection to our sacred center, we will always judge instead of pray.

129.

With Mother Earth,
we can find our path wherever we go.

130.

Only by offering death to those things that cannot serve our highest good can we truly live.

131.

If you've taken offense to it,
you haven't learned the lesson.

132.

The more profound lesson in every situation is always to move from "What THEY are doing to me" to "What they are trying to teach us."

133.

The mistake isn't over until we've forgiven,
learned the lesson, and moved on.

134.

Religion, ideology, and nationalism should never trump
our relationship with Mother Earth.
Mother Earth first.

135.

The Great Consciousness is found
in the seven sacred laws.
Humility, truth, respect, honesty, wisdom,
courage, and love.

136.

The paradox is we don't truly understand love until we offer our healing of Mother Earth to others.

137.

Observation without judgment is
our most incredible wisdom.

138.

When the hearing is blind, the eyes betray us.

139.

Mother EARTH doesn't choose sides.
Neither left nor right. Nor politics.
We, as a species, don't have to choose sides.
But we do have to choose her.

140.

We don't defend the land as much as we assert
our connection to its consciousness.
We are the Earth Consciousness.

141.

Love is knowing we are a part of everything.
Humility is knowing everything is a part of us.

142.

If those voices within you and around you
aren't supporting you, release them.

143.

Our thank you offer is a single expression
of our gratitude.

144.

I am the sum of all I have survived.
I am the sum of all my ancestors who survived.
I am the sum of all Mother Earth has survived.
We are survivors.

145.

I am all the ancestors who carry me.
We are all the ancestors who carry us.

146.

We gather not only because of the Medicine and not only for the Medicine but because we are the Medicine.

147.

Our culture is Mother Earth and
working together as one.

148.

All prayers should begin with Thank You.

149.

Full circle prayer: Loving me is praying for you.

150.

It's normal not to be perfect.

151.

Protection of our children and the next seven generations begins with walking the Red Road, Mother Earth, and the Seven sacred teachings.

152.

We grow spiritually by our relationship with
Mother Earth: Humility, love, truth, honesty, wisdom,
courage, and strength.

153.

The Spiritual paradox is that we find ourselves
by sitting in a circle.

154.

We don't heal by standing around with people
who are uninterested in healing.

155.

If we don't find our truth,
someone else will tell us our truth.

156.

Use everything Creator gave you.

157.

Connect to anything that carries life,
and they will show you the world.

158.

We must believe in all; all life is sacred,
not just a savior or messiah. We are already sacred.

159.

Life wins when we celebrate all life.

160.

Re-indigenize.
Replace the term angels with ancestors.

161.

If we want a good life,
we must celebrate with and for all life.

162.

Sadness, loneliness, and depression are not a disease
but a sign we are disconnecting from
those things that offer life.

163.

Most people aren't under a spiritual attack but are under the influence of a bad attitude and bad choices and consequences from misaligned choices.

164.

Much sadness is unrecognized gratitude.

165.

The Colonial and patriarchal system is based on
lateral violence of being adversarial.

166.

We must become so firmly connected in our power with
Mother Earth and our ancestors that
we can't be intimidated or swayed to hate.

167.

Those who create enemies between us
are all our enemies.

168.

We have come to a new growth and existence when
we understand it's okay not to be okay
but still have the awareness to see, hear, and feel
the beauty of the world around us.

169.

We continue to shape and model ourselves to be
the best ancestors we can be.

170.

Healing:
Let us not be confused between what we did to survive
and who we are trying to become.

171.

Spiritual law:
The way to connect to the stars is first to join
Mother Earth, because you cannot connect up there
until you're all connected down here.

172.

Toxic masculinity is the act of replacing sacred law, like humility, with believing in Him and begging.

173.

Indigenous Spirituality:
Sovereignty and collective rights are
rooted in sacred connection.
Human rights are not truly human until
Mother Earth (M.E.) is honored as part of them.

174.

Your beliefs do not make you a good person;
how you equally treat Mother Earth, animals,
and all other life does.

175.

Like Mother Earth, our human rights
aren't a political issue.

176.

It isn't the root system that creates life for the tree.
It is the relationship between the root and the soil of
Mother Earth that makes life, and all the other life
that interacts with the tree.

177.

Acceptance, change isn't a test; it is a choice.

178.

Medicine, like the sun and the moon,
does not choose sides.

179.

A life lived with the seven sacred teachings
will keep us away from a life of regret.

180.

The struggle is between the illusion of one
and the acceptance of the other.

181.

Intentional inspiration is imagination.

182.

Those who fail to use imagination are lost.

183.

We are dyslexic.
We should be triggered to heal and get healthy
instead of triggered to have anger or fear.

184.

The olds always look for the good
in people's words and actions.

185.

When we pray and call on the Ancestors,
we never pray alone.

186.

Our human collective consciousness is directly linked to our relationships with fire, water, air, and Earth.

187.

For humanity to change, we must start identifying as humans before anything else.

188.

Honoring our life is honoring that
beautiful unknown place within us.

189.

When we pray, we always include the Stars,
Star Nation, and all the constellations.

190.

Consciousness connection is the wisdom
that we are looking for.

191.

Everything in the universe has its own sound and
corresponding frequency.
(Voice = sound = frequency = life)
This is our creation and part of our creation story each
individual is a part of but must find their place
in this frequent circle.

192.

Creator, consciousness and the Universe:
Consciousness is not a linear road but a circle
that creates all things. It has no borders or boundaries.
It does not stop at the outer rings of Earth.
That is just our beginning.

193.

What are our boundaries?
Respecting our truth.
Beginning with: *we are all sacred*.

194.

We as individuals are a beautiful part
of the universal collective consciousness.

195.

The spiritual paradox is that our ancestors are gone
but they never left.

196.

When we are connected to the Earth, there is nothing in this world that we will miss. We will feel at home.

197.

When education is designed to remove our imagination,
it becomes indoctrination.

198.

Religion tells you who you are
solely based on other people's ideas.
Mother Earth tells us we are
a part of something beautiful.

199.

What is love?
Love isn't only our birthright. It is our heritage.

200.

We don't sit with the elements.
We draw near them because we are the elements.

201.

We don't say Mother Earth as a teaching
but as a knowing.

202.

We can use fire, water, air, or EARTH, any one or combination, to guide us in both growth and healing.

203.

Spiritual Stagnation. That place where we cannot see
further than we've grown.

204.

Our duty as humans and to the next seven generations:
Our obligations to all life is to restore balance and
harmony to Mother Earth.

205.

Using kind words helps us find our way home.

206.

The old saying, "accept your abundance,"
means you are a part of this world.

207.

If your belief requires everyone to believe what you believe, it isn't a religion. It is manipulation.

208.

The message is in the Medicine. The Medicine is in the
gathering. The gathering is where the hearts connect.
The heart is where the love is found. Repeat.

209.

Are we listening to the prayers of our ancestors seven
generations previous? Are we living the life
they wanted us to live?

210.

Faith doesn't come from a religion.
It comes from our connection to Mother Earth.

211.

Interpersonal Relationships:
There is only chaos and confusion in loving
someone else before loving yourself.

212.

We only seek to remember the wisdom
that has come before us.

213.

Life is eternal, constantly renewed. Our existence evolves in cycles—what sleeps will awaken, and what awakens will sleep again. The spaces in between hold great and necessary lessons.

214.

As Indigenous, we believe all healing begins with prayer.

215.

One of the medicines of stillness that should be
observed is imagination.

216.

Animals can see what humans cannot.

217.

The water has an intimate knowledge of our physical being and the Spirit that moves within.

218.

Everything is the red road.

219.

When we pray together, you are a part of me;
if you leave, you take a part of me with you.

220.

Clarity is everything. Water is clarity. Air is clarity.
Fire us clarity. Earth is clarity.
We will not know clarity until we are
about each of these.

221.

The visions and prophecies from different tribes and
Medicine men and women are all a part
of the collective consciousness.

222.

They cannot kill the universal consciousness that flows through our ancestors and now through us.

223.

Unity is found in our collective consciousness.
Freedom is found in our collected consciousness.

224.

If we do not understand life and what it offers us, the natural course of understanding is we can never understand death. Both will be foreign and dangerous concepts. We will be spiritually naïve and open to believing fearful and false narratives.

225.

Consciousness will be the sound of
Medicine in the future.

226.

When humanity understands that all nations, circles, and tribes, which include the standing nations, the fish nations, the winged, and the four-legged, are all sons and daughters of Earth, we will know peace.
Until then, no peace.

227.

Medicine Wheel teaching:
Our belief, understanding, and connection to
Mother Earth expedites our healing.

228.

We must learn to accept our imagination
to meet the unknown.

229.

We are confused about when we are supposed to be listening and when we are supposed to be responding.

230.

The laws of the universe are, in fact, universal.
They are all around us our entire lives.
Begging for a relationship with us.

231.

Our connection to the Earth is what connects us
to the sky.

232.

Mother Earth is a language and prayer
we all understand.

233.

Be mindful when talking: Mother Earth, the Ancestors, the next seven generations, and the universe always listen and respond.

234.

We, as Indigenous people of Earth, do not seek
attention but only respect for Mother Earth.

235.

When we are grateful for our life, we show others
it is okay to be thankful for theirs.

236.

Being yourself costs nothing.
Not being yourself may cost you everything.

237.

When we begin to return to the natural order
and alignment with Mother Earth,
peace will begin to return to humanity.

238.

Every direction of the Medicine Wheel offers us a message of healing, new life, and new beginnings.

239.

It is hard to detox without Mother Earth.
Emotionally authentic healing comes from all
directions, just like life and the winds of wisdom.

240.

The attention of the self includes Earth
and all her medicines.

241.

When we communicate with flowers, we begin to understand that not only do we bloom from the inside but long before when we were only seeds.

242.

Wisdom is reflecting on and taking all perspectives
into account. The seven directions, including and
especially the next seven generations,
and being accountable for all.

243.

Remembering we are Earth is the highest form
of learning and listening.

244.

Stillness is a portal to peace.
Silence is a portal to serenity.

245.

The best investment I make to humanity,
Mother Earth, the ancestors, the next
seven generations, and myself is to work on
myself and become a better version of myself.

246.

Gratitude is the Sunrise.
We are to make an offering and invest spiritually into
this gratitude by carrying it with us throughout the day.

247.

The beauty that is part of everything is the mystery
that lies within.

248.

The prayers we carry and the way we walk with them
always reveal our wounds and our healing,
who we are, and what we believe in.

249.

Prayers are our way back home to our sacred center.

250.

Silence through stillness. Stillness through serenity.

251.

Do you want to know how you will understand love?
What is your relationship with, and
how are you treating her?

252.

Alignment with life begins with Gratitude.
Let us learn to thank the Creator for everything
before we ask for anything.

253.

The spiritual paradox is that our ability to be vulnerable
is our greatest strength.

254.

When we see more with our eyes closed,
our life has just begun.

255.

All prayers are our offering to
the next seven generations.

256.

Our spiritual awareness, what we see, hear, and comprehend, equals our level of healing.

257.

When we speak using loving and kind words,
we begin to heal all who listen.

258.

Our boundaries aren't the only thing,
they are everything.

259.

War has no peace. Peace has no war.
Peace doesn't choose sides.

260.

The original trauma is humanity's severed relationships
and connection with Mother Earth.

261.

Life begins with forgiveness.
Everything brings death.

262.

Global peace begins when we treat
Mother Earth peacefully.

263.

The first battle we stop is the one
we fight with ourselves.

264.

Air, Water, Fire, and Earth.
If we are not connected to the elements outside of us,
how can we expect the elements inside of us
to be in balance.

265.

Our spiritual sovereignty begins with living the ways of Earth. Understanding her interconnectedness to all things, only then will humanity begin to understand our place in this world.

266.

We each have our own unique frequency.
It is our spiritual fingerprint.

267.

The language we need to hear is
in the next breath that we take.

268.

Spiritual law:
We are always heard. Everything we don't say,
the next seven generations hear.

269.

Finding beauty is looking for those voices unspoken
in those places unlooked.

270.

Our Spiritual integrity is based on
our ability to speak our truth.

271.

The spiritual paradox is that there can be no
vulnerability without courage.

272.

How do we connect to Mother Earth?
Be grateful for life.
How do we connect to love?
Be grateful for life.

273.

The one who can't find gratitude is lost.
The one who finds things to be grateful for is growing.
The one who is grateful for everything has arrived.

274.

Abundance is a work attitude.
Not a begging opportunity.

275.

Air Medicine:
The voice that we are first looking for is our own.
Our own sacred wind is sacred, aka breath.

276.

As Mother Earth is both Mother and Grandmother,
each season is a relative and ancestor.

277.

We are all human.
We are all pieces of the truth.
But to find ourselves, we have to speak and
live our truth.

278.

Humility knows the way to the truth.
The truth knows the way to Love.
Love knows the way to find you.

279.

Prayer is the beginning of all abundance.

280.

Comprehension is not a prerequisite for
spiritual connection or growth.

281.

If we listen to the seasons, they tell us to
time, relax, change, and replenish.

282.

Love is offering our truth.

283.

In the realm of the Spirit, the beauty of this world
is found where you do not want to look.

284.

Definition of Abundance:
Abundance is absolutely doing what you need to do
at the exact moment you need to do it.

285.

All we are is consciousness.
Either we deepen it and learn or suffer if we don't.

286.

We don't die here, we only wake up in the next world.

287.

Our capacity to heal is based on
our ability to be truthful.
Our ability to be truthful depends on
our ability to be vulnerable.
Without vulnerability, there can be no healing.

288.

Above all be loyal to the truth.

289.

Civilizations rise and fall with the language they choose to speak and their relationship with Mother Earth.

290.

Gratitude:
Gratitude is our gateway to healing and happiness.

291.

Love includes the presence of patience;
if it does not, it is incomplete.

292.

Spiritual agreement 101:
Maintain gratitude.
If we cannot manage our gratitude,
it's nobody's fault but our own.

293.

External versus Internal:
Misalignment brings fear.

294.

The birthplace of alignment is the seven Grandfather teachings. The birthplace of Passion is right after this.

295.

The mind will replay what the heart hasn't learned.

296.

The size of the mountain depends on
the amount of resistance.

297.

The truth is finding out who you are
is what you're doing when no one is looking.
The truth is what you say when no one is listening

298.

We are born.
We come from our children.
We come from that place where I remember you.
We come from the helpers.
We come from Earth.
We come from the Stars.
We have come full circle.
We wake up.

299.

If Mother Earth is from the stars, then so are we.

300.

We are always preparing for the great oneness.

301.

We are not only the elements,
we are to speak on behalf of them as well.

302.

It's hard to grow, emotionally, mentally, spiritually, and physically when we aren't part of those allies, guides, and partners that help us grow emotionally, mentally, spiritually, and physically. Mother Earth.

303.

If our healing doesn't include an intimate relationship
with Mother Earth, then it is incomplete.

304.

Humility is a spiritual law. Offering tobacco is humility.

305.

Our relationship with the water is both internal and external. Seen and unseen.

306.

Without our relationship with Mother Earth, we will forget life is most important. She teaches us all life is beautiful and necessary.

307.

The issue: patriarchal colonial religions do not protect life. Patriarchal colonial religions protect themselves.

308.

We inherit our sacred breath from our ancestors,
and we breathe and offer it to our unborn
and the next seven generations.

309.

Toxic people are misaligned with something other than those life-giving forces. They are always feeding.

310.

The greatest spiritual insight is found in our ability to help others. This is twofold. One helps the other in deepening our insight, strengthening urban vision to be able to see beyond where we could see before.

311.

Part of making good relations is understanding,
creating, and honoring healthy boundaries.

312.

Humility is stillness and silence
within the crisis and chaos.

313.

Life:
The greater commitment to life, love, honesty, wisdom,
respect, truth, courage and humility,
the greater the reward.
The reward:
happiness, serenity, calm mind and peaceful heart.

314.

The paradox is celebrating peace
is celebrating each other.

315.

We cannot live our truth if we are living in blame, shame, and guilt. Stop it.

316.

How do we heal the Earth?
Connect to it.
How do we change ourselves?
Connect to the Earth.
How do we heal?
Connect to both.

317.

No one is supposed to tell or guide your story but you.

318.

Humanity will always struggle with the illusion of separation from each other and all other life until we accept and walk with Mother Earth's consciousness.

319.

The only thing confusing about the truth is not living it.
Humility, honesty, love, courage, respect, and wisdom.

320.

Humanity's first lost memory is that
we are all brothers and sisters.

321.

Humanity:
Remember, we are supposed to leave this world
better than we found it.

322.

Lower consciousness believes and creates separation.
Higher consciousness believes and creates unity.

323.

Our physical connection to the land is found
in our unseen connection to Spirit.

324.

Those who wish to live an amazing life
connected to spiritual health:
1. Step outside your comfort zone.
2. Stop lying, speak the truth.
3. Stop blaming and shame guilting yourself.

325.

Poverty isn't a physical experience but begins as a spiritual experience. Based solely on acting and living out of alignment with abundance not creating, acting or taking the opportunities offered.

326.

Let us go to that place where prayers meet.

327.

In life, there are no tests.
Gratitude cancels blame, shame, and guilt.
Let us choose wisely.

328.

Abundance, like prayer, isn't based on begging.
It's based on timely and right action.

329.

Fire, air, water, and Mother Earth.
If we sit with the elements of life long enough,
they will show us their dreams.
This offering is a gift of life for us.

330.

If you cannot see the beauty of our Mother Earth,
that's not anybody's fault but your own.
Beauty is everywhere. Seasons, sunset, sunrise, trees,
flowers, oceans, rivers, stars, everything.

331.

Medicine Wheel:
Human intimate relationships.
We have to learn to be comfortable in our own silence
and stillness before we engage in a relationship
with any other.

332.

Ancient sacred agreement.
The truth. How we avoid confusion and conflict.

333.

What is life? Our commitment to it.

334.

Whether we understand, like it or not,
we are our relationship with all the elements.

335.

Medicine Wheel teaching:
The birthplace of Mother Earth is the Stars.

336.

It is traditional to give thanks every day.

337.

Indigenous Spiritual protocol dictates the understanding that we accept we live in two worlds at the same time, interwoven and overlapping, seen and unseen. Physical and spiritual.

338.

We never understand a multidimensional consciousness with a singular religious consciousness. This one-dimensional idea will keep us separated not only from our true selves but from the rest of our multiverse.

339.

The spiritual paradox is that our physical foundation is
built with a relationship with the unseen.

340.

Our new directions and horizons begin with the unseen. Then, that means our new spiritual destination is a new consciousness.

341.

Religion = unconscious.
Spiritual = awakened and aware.
Consciousness = natural state.

342.

Understanding our new consciousness.
Without imagination, there is no consciousness.

343.

We are the people of Earth. A beautiful people.
Nothing more and nothing less.
When we start realizing this, a new dawn and
new humanity have begun.

344.

Awareness:
In a brilliant and deadly manipulation move,
colonial religious bodies removed our Indigenous seven
sacred Grandfather laws and replaced them with the
seven deadly sins.

345.

One prayer, one heart, one ceremony is Mother Earth.

346.

Journey to awareness and connect to things unseen.
We must go beyond what we do not know,
we must do what we do not understand.

347.

Silence and stillness around us are not prerequisites
for silence and stillness on the Inside.

348.

Prayer:
It is understanding the spiritual flow. The natural
rhythms, harmony, and cycles of the world around us.
Seasons, Mother Earth, and Stars.

349.

We begin to connect to the natural sacred agreement
of life when we refuse to hate.

350.

It will always be the ones with a healthy relationship with Mother Earth who will bring peace and serenity not only to themselves but to the world.

351.

We are to bring the people back to the medicine of
Mother Earth and the medicine of unity.
This will bring the people of all nations, circles,
and tribes back to the forgotten ancient agreement
of oneness.

352.

Those who do not have good relations with the Spirit, like humility, truth, honesty, respect, wisdom, courage, and love, will use words to divide the people and will not conduct themselves in a way that brings unity.

353.

Those who take offence to unkind words
have yet to find harmony in theirs.

354.

We as humans are incapable of fully understanding the Creator's Love. To help us understand, the Creator has given us the gift of helping others. When we help others, we begin to understand and experience love.

355.

Indigenous like the Medicine
The wheel isn't about color, it's about responsibility
and connection to Mother Earth.

356.

Every prayer gives hope to the next seven generations.

357.

Those healings we avoid,
including those things we do not talk about,
will be passed on to our children to deal with.

358.

Our love from the individual to the rest of humanity
should include the stars and the star nations;
if it does not, it is incomplete.

359.

We continually find ourselves
by honoring our boundaries.

360.

There can be no peace on Earth until the people of
Earth decide to be at peace with Earth.
We must stop treating her like a resource and start
treating her like a relative.

361.

Creator, Great Spirit, help me listen in quiet ways.
Especially in those moments when quiet
is not within me or around me.

362.

Silence begins within.
Until then, nothing is silent.

363.

Is how you feel aligned with what you deserve?
Is any of this aligned with the life-offering
sources of Mother Earth?

364.

If we are not connected to those things that offer us life,
air, water, fire, Earth, how can we possibly understand
who we are and what we are supposed to do
with the life we are to live?

365.

The Stars and the Star Nations are part of our home.

366.

The difference between asking and begging is humility.

367.

Gratitude is a superpower.
It is a close relative to gentleness. Cousin to compassion.

About the Author

Wayne William Snellgrove, a Saulteaux Indian, was born on Fishing Lake First Nation Reserve in Saskatchewan. He is a modern-day genocide survivor of the Canadian government's policy of assimilation known as The 60s Scoop, a two-time USA National swimming champion and a USA Swimming National Team member. He is also the author of *Daily Medicine, Whispers from the Hollow Bone*, and *Sifting Through the Ashes*.